NATIONAL FOOTBALL LEAGUE

SUPER BOWL
SUPER TOUCHDOWNS

NFL

by JOE LAYDEN

SCHOLASTIC INC.

New York   Toronto   London   Auckland   Sydney
Mexico City   New Delhi   Hong Kong   Buenos Aires

ISBN 0-439-82815-5

Published by Scholastic Inc. SCHOLASTIC and associated logos
are trademarks and/or registered trademarks of Scholastic Inc.

12 11 10 9 8 7 6 5 4 3 2   6 7 8 9 10/0

Designed by Michael Malone
Printed in the U.S.A.
First printing, August 2006

There's something about the Super Bowl that brings out the best in an athlete.

Football's biggest game, played on its grandest stage, encourages its participants to perform at the absolute peak of their abilities. The Super Bowl has become a "Super Show," with millions of people tuning in from all over the world. And more often than not, the players live up to their promise and succeed in delivering brilliant performances, in a game that lingers in the memory long after the final gun has sounded.

Hines Ward

EACH YEAR there are superstars who reinforce their reputations by playing magnificently in the Super Bowl. And there are newcomers who step out of the shadows and into the spotlight with a single great game

Willie Parker

. . . or maybe just a single great play. In the end, we remember the touchdowns more vividly than anything else. We recall images of a pass floating through the air and into the hands of a wide receiver, and of the wild celebration that follows his arrival in the end zone. It's true that there have been blowouts in the Super Bowl. It's also true that there have been thrilling finishes in which placekickers have decided the outcome. But it's especially true that the NFL's most important game has produced more than its share of spectacular touchdowns, some of which determined the winner, and some of which merely caused us to shake our heads in awe. On the following pages are some of the most memorable TDs in Super Bowl history. Some were scored by offensive players. Others were scored by defenders or kick return specialists. But they all have one thing in common: They helped elevate the Super Bowl to new heights!

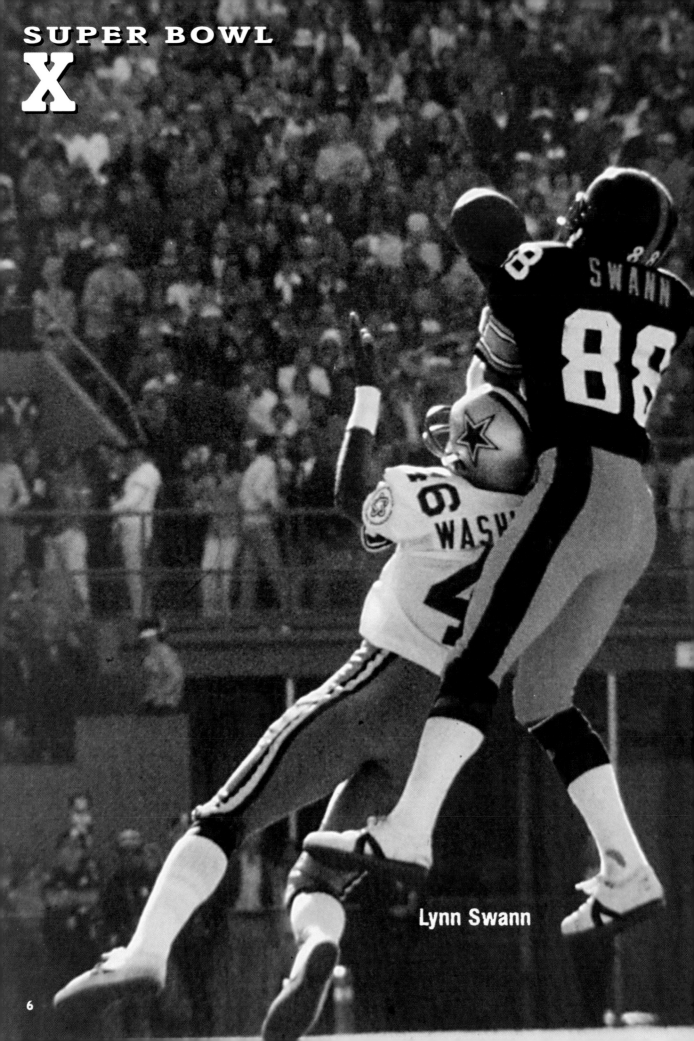

Lynn Swann

As Graceful as a Swann

THE GREAT Pittsburgh Steelers teams of the 1970s were known primarily for their vaunted defense, appropriately nicknamed "The Steel Curtain." But on this particular Super Bowl Sunday, it was offense that stole the show, and the outstanding performer was Lynn Swann. Few people expected Swann to be at his best against the Cowboys. He had spent two nights in a hospital recovering from a concussion sustained during the Steelers' AFC championship game victory over the Oakland Raiders. Just one day before the Super Bowl, he admitted to feeling weak and disoriented; he even dropped a few passes in the team's final practice session. In the case of Lynn Swann, though, appearances could be deceiving. One of the NFL's all-time great receivers, he was as tough as he was elegant. True, Swann could soar over defenders and outrun almost any defensive back, but he also knew how to catch the ball in traffic. And no one was better at coming up with big plays. One of the biggest of his career came with just over three minutes remaining in Super Bowl X, and the Steelers clinging to a 15–10 lead. From his own 36-yard line, quarterback Terry Bradshaw dropped back to pass on third down. Most teams would have settled for a short pass, but the Steelers went for broke —and hit paydirt! Swann angled across the middle, got a step behind cornerback Mark Washington, and then shifted into a higher gear. He hauled in a perfect strike from Bradshaw, right in stride, inside the Dallas 10-yard line, and then jogged into the end zone. Bradshaw, who was hit hard just as he released the ball, never saw the result. But Swann's 64-yard touchdown reception sealed Pittsburgh's victory. Combined with a leaping 53-yard reception earlier in the game, it also assured Swann of a Super Bowl MVP trophy.

Terry Bradshaw

Dallas COWBOYS	7	3	0	7	17
Pittsburgh STEELERS	7	0	0	14	21

SCORING

DAL-D. Pearson 29 pass from Staubach (Fritsch kick)
PIT-Grossman 7 pass from Bradshaw (Gerela kick)
DAL- FG Fritsch 36
PIT- safety Harrison 0
PIT- FG Gerela 36
PIT- FG Gerela 18
PIT- Swann 64 pass from Bradshaw (kick failed)
DAL- P. Howard 34 pass from Staubach (Fritsch kick)

John Riggins

Fourth-and-One

MORE THAN 100,000 football fans filled the Rose Bowl in Pasadena for Super Bowl XVII—and every one of them knew what was about to happen. It was early in the fourth quarter and the Washington Redskins were trailing the Miami Dolphins by a score of 17–13. On fourth down from the Miami 43-yard line, just one yard shy of a first down, was there any other call to make? Of course not. The Redskins had to maintain possession if they were going to win, and the man most likely to get that final, hard-earned bit of turf was fullback John Riggins, one of the toughest and most dependable running backs ever to put on a football uniform. So there was no debate. The Redskins knew Riggins would get the ball. The Dolphins knew it. The whole stadium knew it. Millions of fans watching on television knew it. Sometimes, though, the biggest surprise is no surprise at all. Quarterback Joe Theismann took the snap from center and did exactly what he was supposed to do: He handed the ball to Riggins. Instead of just crashing into a

Joe Theismann

wall of blockers and falling forward, the muscular fullback found a gaping hole in the line of scrimmage. Riggins had always been much quicker than most fullbacks, and soon he was deep into the Miami secondary, outrunning linebackers and cornerbacks. One yard became ten, ten became twenty, and suddenly Riggins was in the end zone. He had done the unthinkable. He had taken a simple fourth-and-one play and turned it into a 43-yard touchdown run—at the time, the longest in Super Bowl history. The Dolphins never recovered, and the Redskins went on to a ten-point victory. Riggins, who had come out of retirement just two years earlier, recorded one of the most spectacular rushing performances the Super Bowl had ever seen. It wasn't just that he gained 166 yards and scored the deciding touchdown. It was the fact that he carried the ball 38 times! Riggins, of course, was named MVP. Could there have been any other choice?

Miami DOLPHINS	7	10	0	0	17
Washington REDSKINS	0	10	3	14	27

SCORING

MIA-Cefalo 76 pass from Woodley (Von Schamann kick)
WAS-FG Moseley 31
MIA-FG Von Schamann 20
WAS-Garrett 4 pass from Theismann (Moseley kick)
MIA-Walker 98 kick return (Von Schamann kick)
WAS-FG Moseley 20
WAS-Riggins 43 run (Moseley kick)
WAS-Brown 6 pass from Theismann (Moseley kick)

Marcus Allen

Marcus Sparks the Silver & Black

ON PAPER, this was a dream of a matchup. A Super Bowl worthy of all the hype and hysteria. On one side of the field were the Redskins, who had repeated as NFC champions and looked more than capable of winning a second straight Super Bowl title. They were a team loaded with offensive talent and defensive strength. Washington had an oversized offensive line known as the "Hogs," and a group of small but speedy receivers known as the "Smurfs." They had Joe Theismann at quarterback and John Riggins, the previous year's MVP, at running back. It's no wonder that the Redskins were considered a slight favorite—after all, they had already beaten the AFC champion Raiders during the regular season. But this was a different day and a different game, and it belonged completely to the high-flying Raiders. In a stunning display of offensive power, Los Angeles set a Super Bowl record for points and margin of victory. A game that was supposed to be a nail-biter instead turned out to be a yawner, thanks mainly to the spectacular play of Marcus Allen. The Raiders' running back picked up 191 yards on 20 carries to shatter the Super Bowl rushing record set by Riggins one year earlier. If any single play characterized the lopsided nature of the game, and the way in which fortune seemed to be shining on the Raiders, it was one that featured Allen. On the final play of the third quarter, from the Los Angeles 26-yard line, Allen took a handoff from quarterback Jim Plunkett and tried to follow his blockers on a sweep around the left end. When confronted by a swarm of Washington defenders, Allen reversed direction, then found a hole in the middle of the line. Like a comet, Allen streaked into the Washington secondary, leaving a trail of stunned and helpless defenders flailing in his wake. His 74-yard TD run set a record for the longest run from scrimmage. Funny thing: When he came out of college, some people had suggested that Allen lacked the speed to be an NFL tailback. On this day, though, he was the one man who no one on the Redskins could catch.

Washington REDSKINS	0	3	6	0	9
L.A. RAIDERS	7	14	14	3	38

SCORING

LA-Jensen 0 blocked punt return (Bahr kick)
LA-Branch 12 pass from Plunkett (Bahr kick)
WAS-FG Moseley 24
LA-Squirek 5 interception return (Bahr kick)
WAS-Riggins 1 run (kick blocked)
LA-Allen 5 run (Bahr kick)
LA-Allen 74 run (Bahr kick)
LA-FG Bahr 21

William Perry

The Fridge Is Running

RARELY HAS A PROFESSIONAL SPORTS team captured the public's imagination the way the Chicago Bears did in the fall of 1985. Chasing their first NFL title in more than 50 years, the Bears used a combination of talent, ambition, and personality to achieve a unique place in sports history. They had an undersized, maverick of a quarterback named Jim McMahon. They had one of the NFL's all-time great running

Chicago BEARS	13	10	21	2	46
New England PATRIOTS	3	0	0	7	10

backs in Walter Payton. And they had an unyielding defense led by All-Pro defensive end Richard Dent, the Super Bowl MVP. At the helm of this ship was Mike Ditka, one of the toughest and most demanding coaches ever to walk the sidelines of the NFL. The Bears were so popular that the team even recorded a hit song and video known as "The Super Bowl Shuffle." And the star of the show, without question, was William "The Refrigerator" Perry, a lovable 320-pound rookie defensive lineman with a smile as wide as Chicago's Soldier Field. The Fridge was a capable defender, but it was when he moved to the other side of the ball that the game really got interesting. Fans loved watching Perry line up at fullback, where he was used primarily as a mountainous blocker for Payton. Sometimes, though, he was given an opportunity to run with the ball. That's what happened on Super Bowl Sunday. Late in the third quarter, with the Bears at the New England 1-yard line and already holding a comfortable 37–3 lead, Perry entered the game. He took a handoff from McMahon and rumbled into the end zone, as the crowd at the Superdome in New Orleans went wild. "We had practiced that play during the week," Fridge later explained. "When we got down to the goal line, Coach called me over and said, 'Big guy, here's your chance.' So he put me in and there it was. I scored in the Super Bowl."

SCORING

NE-FG Franklin 36
CHI-FG Butler 28
CHI-FG Butler 24
CHI-Suhey 11 run (Butler kick)
CHI-McMahon 2 run (Butler kick)
CHI-FG Butler 24
CHI-McMahon 1 run (Butler kick)
CHI-Phillips 28 interception return (Butler kick)
CHI-Perry 1 run (Butler kick)
NE-Fryar 8 pass from Grogan (Franklin kick)
CHI-safety Waechter 0

Green Bay PACKERS	35
Kansas City CHIEFS	10

A SUPER STARR

THERE WAS A TIME when the Super Bowl wasn't even known as the Super Bowl. The Packers were the champions of the established National Football League, while the Chiefs were the best in the upstart American Football League. So the game was called the AFL-NFL World Championship. Not until three years later would someone come up with the clever idea of calling it the Super Bowl.

SUPER BOWL I

Nevertheless, the Packers are considered the first Super Bowl champions, thanks mainly to the terrific play of quarterback Bart Starr. The game's Most Valuable Player was a cool QB who rarely missed an open receiver. The Pack, as they are known, overwhelmed the Chiefs that day at Memorial Coliseum in Los Angeles behind a typically flawless performance by Starr. He completed 16 of 23 passes for 250 yards and three touchdowns. The most memorable TD, of course, was the first. After all, there can be only one "first" Super Bowl touchdown, and this one was unforgettable. It came in the first quarter, at a time when the Chiefs were still clinging to the belief that they might have a chance to pull off an upset. Starr dropped back to pass and found wide receiver Max McGee open in the Kansas City secondary. His acrobatic, one-handed grab of Starr's pass resulted in a 37-yard touchdown and gave the Packers an early lead. By the end of the day McGee would have seven receptions for 138 yards, and the Packers would be world champions!

Doug Williams

Poise Under Pressure

SOMETIMES ADVERSITY can bring out the best in an athlete. Consider the case of Doug Williams, quarterback for the Washington Redskins. In the days leading up to Super Bowl XXII, Williams was asked to shoulder multiple burdens. Of course, any quarterback playing on football's biggest stage is under pressure, but Williams' situation was unique. He was the first African-American to start at quarterback in the Super Bowl, and much of the media interest surrounding the game focused on precisely that fact. Like it or not—and he preferred not to make a big deal about it—Williams was breaking new ground. On top of that, he was playing with a whopper of a headache, thanks to a bad tooth that required root canal work just one day before the Super Bowl. For a while it seemed that a storybook season would have a lousy ending for Williams and the Redskins. They fell behind 10–0 in the first quarter, and when Williams twisted his knee a few minutes later, Denver appeared to have the game in hand. But

Washington REDSKINS	0	35	0	7	42
Denver BRONCOS	10	0	0	0	10

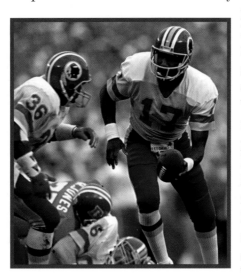

Williams responded with one of the most brilliant performances in Super Bowl history. He shook off the injury and sparked an offensive barrage like nothing the Super Bowl had ever seen. It began spectacularly. Williams fired a bomb to his speediest receiver, Ricky Sanders, who had streaked past the Broncos' defense. Sanders took the pass in full flight and sprinted into the end zone for an 80-yard touchdown! It was a play that stunned the Broncos and instantly turned the tide of the game. Before the second quarter was over, Williams had thrown three more touchdown passes, and the Redskins had a 35–10 lead. Needless to say, Denver never recovered. The Redskins rolled to their second Super Bowl championship, and Williams was voted the game's Most Valuable Player. He completed 18 of 29 passes for a Super Bowl record 340 yards. More importantly, he demonstrated with uncommon poise that the color of a man's skin has absolutely no bearing on his strength of character.

SCORING

DEN-Nattiel 56 pass from Elway (Karlis kick)
DEN-FG Karlis 24
WAS-Sanders 80 pass from D. Williams (Haji-Sheikh kick)
WAS-Clark 27 pass from D. Williams (Haji-Sheikh kick)
WAS-Smith 58 run (Haji-Sheikh kick)
WAS-Sanders 50 pass from D. Williams (Haji-Sheikh kick)
WAS-Didier 8 pass from D. Williams (Haji-Sheikh kick)
WAS-Smith 4 run (Haji-Sheikh kick)

Ricky Sanders

| Miami DOLPHINS | 14 |
| Washington REDSKINS | 7 |

WHY KICKERS SHOULD STICK TO KICKING

NO ONE COULD HANDLE the Miami Dolphins that season. With a potent ground game led by fullback Larry Csonka and tailback Jim Kiick, and a passing attack that featured quarterback Bob Griese and wide receiver Paul Warfield, Miami knew how to put points on the scoreboard. The defense wasn't bad, either. As a matter of fact, safety Jake Scott was the MVP of Super Bowl VII, a game the Dolphins controlled from the beginning. It wasn't until very late in the game that the Redskins got on the scoreboard, thanks to one of the strangest plays in Super Bowl history. Holding a 14–0 lead, Miami lined up for a field goal. But the Redskins blocked the attempt by kicker Garo Yepremian. And that's when the fun began. At only 5-foot-8, Yepremian was the smallest man on the field, but that did not stop him from scooping up the loose ball and trying to salvage the play. Yepremian took a few awkward steps, then decided to throw the ball. Unfortunately for Miami, Yepremian wasn't much of a quarterback. The ball wobbled off his fingertips—it was ultimately ruled a fumble, rather than a pass—and into the waiting arms of Washington defender Mike Bass, who ran 49 yards for the touchdown. By then, however, only two minutes remained in the game. The Dolphins were able to run out the clock and capture their first Super Bowl championship. They finished the season with a perfect 17–0 record, an accomplishment no team has matched.

SUPER BOWL VII

© Mike Powell/NFL Photos

Joe Montana

Super Joe Does It Again!

THERE IS SO MUCH anticipation leading up to the Super Bowl that it's almost impossible for the game to meet expectations. Once in a while, though, it equals or surpasses all of the hype. Super Bowl XXIII, played at Joe Robbie Stadium in Miami, was such a game. The 49ers, who were favored to win their third Super Bowl, got everything they could handle from the AFC champion Bengals. In fact, when Jim Breech kicked his third field goal of the day with just 3:20 left in the game, Cincinnati had a 16–13 lead. The 49ers were in serious trouble. Then again, this was a team that knew how to score points in a hurry, with a quarterback who seemed to be at his very best when the pressure was high. There's a reason Joe Montana is in the Hall of Fame, and it was never more apparent than on San Francisco's final possession of the game. Montana had been in this situation before, in 1982, when he guided the 49ers to a thrilling, last-second victory over the Cowboys in the NFC title game.

John Taylor

So it was not surprising to see Montana work his magic once again. Time after time he dropped back and released passes with pinpoint accuracy. There was a beautiful 27-yard completion to Jerry Rice, the game's MVP, that gave the 49ers a first down at the Cincinnati 18-yard line. And then an 8-yard completion to Roger Craig, who had circled out of the backfield to get open. That set up the biggest play of the game, and one of the most memorable TDs in Super Bowl history. As Montana barked out signals, Rice went in motion from right to left. The Bengals naturally focused on Rice, one of the NFL's most dangerous receivers. But on this play he was merely a decoy. The target was Rice's counterpart at wide receiver, John Taylor, who jumped off the line of scrimmage, faked out a defender, and crossed into the middle of the field. Montana found him, of course, and with just 34 seconds showing on the clock, Taylor scored the winning touchdown. For the third time in the 1980s, the 49ers were world champions!

Cincinnati BENGALS	0	3	10	3	16
San Francisco 49ERS	3	0	3	14	20

SCORING

SF- FG Cofer 41
CIN-FG Breech 34
CIN-FG Breech 43
SF- FG Cofer 32
CIN-Jennings 93 kick return (Breech kick)
SF-Rice 14 pass from Montana (Cofer kick)
CIN-FG Breech 40
SF-Taylor 10 pass from Montana (Cofer kick)

Emmitt Smith

Cowboy Up

WHEN EMMITT SMITH first arrived in the NFL, it was tempting to suggest that he might not last too long. He stood only 5-feet-9 inches tall, hardly big enough to withstand the pounding that a professional running back can expect to endure. But height told only a portion of the story. Smith carried more than 200 pounds on his compact, muscular frame. He was blessed with outstanding speed and an uncanny ability to evade defenders. He would cut so sharply and suddenly that tacklers would be left grasping at nothing but air. And, of course, there were the traits you couldn't see, like intelligence and character. And heart. All of these things helped make Smith one of the greatest running backs the NFL has ever seen. In 2002 he surpassed the legendary Walter Payton to become the league's all-time leading rusher. But it was during the early 1990s, when "America's Team" dominated the NFL, that Smith was at his best. The Cowboys won three Super Bowls in a span of four years, from 1992 to 1995. Smith played a major role in each of those victories, but it was in Super Bowl XXVIII that he truly left his mark. Playing tireless and

Dallas COWBOYS	6	0	14	10	30
Buffalo BILLS	3	10	0	0	13

fearless football, Smith carried the ball 30 times for 132 yards and two touchdowns as the Cowboys overpowered the Buffalo Bills for the second straight year. An amazing nineteen of his carries came in the second half, as Dallas decided to simply put the ball in Smith's hands and let him run out the clock. The decisive play of the game occurred midway through the third quarter, with the score tied, 13–13. Following a Buffalo punt, Smith carried the ball six consecutive times for 46 yards. He took a one-play break while fullback Daryl Johnston caught a three-yard pass, then went back to work. And what a job he did! At the Buffalo 15-yard line, Smith took a handoff from quarterback Troy Aikman. What began as an ordinary running play quickly developed into one of the Super Bowl's most enduring images. One after another, Buffalo defenders tried to stop Smith. But no one could bring him down. Five times he shed tacklers. The Bills bounced off him as though he were made of rubber. Smith's engine finally cooled when he was in the end zone, with the ball safely tucked under his arm, and the game in hand.

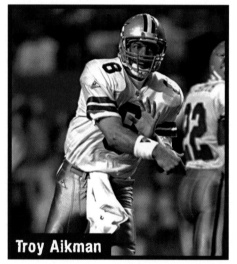

Troy Aikman

SCORING

DAL-FG Murray 41
BUF-FG Christie 54
DAL-FG Murray 24
BUF-Thomas 4 run (Christie kick)
BUF-FG Christie 28
DAL-Washington 46 def. fumble rec. (Murray kick)
DAL-E. Smith 15 run (Murray kick)
DAL-E. Smith 1 run (Murray kick)
DAL-FG Murray 20

SUPER BOWL
XXIX

Steve Young

Young Gets His Chance

NO ATHLETE has ever displayed more patience and maturity than Steve Young. Although he was one of the top collegiate players in the country, and came to the 49ers as an established professional quarterback with impeccable skills, Young spent his first few years in San Francisco on the bench. Why? Simple. The 49ers already had a pretty good starting QB named Joe Montana. Young wasn't happy about his role as a backup, but he accepted it quietly and professionally. He studied Montana, one of the game's all-time greats, and he waited for his opportunity. When the time came for him to step into a starting role, Young was ready. But it wasn't until Super Bowl XXIX, at Joe Robbie Stadium in Miami, that Young finally emerged as a truly great quarterback in his own right. On that day he rewrote the Super Bowl record book, completing 24 of 36 passes for 325 yards and six touchdowns as the 49ers won their fifth championship. No one had ever thrown six TD passes in a single Super Bowl. Not even Joe Montana. But Young was unstoppable. He didn't throw a single interception, despite filling the air with passes. He even rushed for 49 yards. From the opening kick-off, Young made it obvious that this was going to be his day. On San Francisco's very first possession, less than a minute and a half into the game, Young tossed a beautiful 44-yard touchdown pass to give the 49ers a 7–0 lead. His target was Jerry Rice, who had long been a favorite of Montana's as well. As Rice strode into the end zone, Young pumped his fist. There would be other perfect strikes before the day was over, including a 51-yard touchdown pass to running back Ricky Watters. But it was the first TD that mattered most, for that one made it clear: The torch had been passed to the next generation!

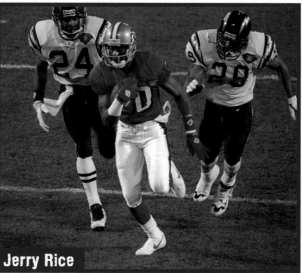

Jerry Rice

San Diego CHARGERS	7	3	8	8	26
San Francisco 49ERS	14	14	14	7	49

SCORING

SF-Rice 44 pass from S. Young (Brien kick)
SF-Watters 51 pass from S. Young (Brien kick)
SD-Means 1 run (Carney kick)
SF-Floyd 5 pass from S. Young (Brien kick)
SF-Watters 8 pass from S. Young (Brien kick)
SD-FG Carney 31
SF-Watters 9 run (Brien kick)
SF-Rice 15 pass from S. Young (Brien kick)
SD-Coleman 98 kick return (2-pt Seay from Humphries)
SF-Rice 7 pass from S. Young (Brien kick)
SD-Martin 30 pass from Humphries (2-pt Pupunu from Humphries)

Desmond Howard

Desmond Runs to Glory

BY THE TIME he reached the Louisiana Superdome on Super Bowl Sunday, Desmond Howard was far removed from his glory days at the University of Michigan. In 1991 Howard had been awarded the Heisman Trophy, presented annually to the best player in college football. He was a wiry, acrobatic wide receiver then, with a slender frame that seemed almost too delicate for the game of football. And, in fact, the more muscular professional game played in the NFL was a difficult adjustment for Howard. After bouncing around the league for a few years, he landed in Green Bay as a free agent and settled comfortably into a new role as a kick return specialist. With his quiet confidence and gritty play, quarterback Brett Favre was the undisputed leader of the Packers. But Desmond Howard was the team's most explosive player. He could single-handedly alter the course of a game, as he did against the Patriots in Super Bowl XXXI. Even now, nearly a decade later, the numbers are hard to fathom. Howard returned four kickoffs for 154 yards. He added 90 yards on four punt returns for a total of 244 return yards. It's no wonder that New England defensive coordinator Al Groh said afterward, "Desmond Howard ruined a perfectly good football game." It was meant to be a compliment, of course. Football is typically a game won or lost in the trenches, along the line of scrimmage. But Howard, the game's MVP, changed all of that. He put on a one-man show, electrifying the crowd of more than 72,000 with spectacular bursts of speed and dazzling moves. The highlight of the game came late in the third quarter, after Curtis Martin's 18-yard touchdown run brought the Patriots to within six points of the Packers. Thanks to Howard, though, New England's excitement was short-lived. He took the ensuing kickoff at the one-yard line, and quickly found a hole in the New England coverage. Within seconds Howard had shifted into a higher gear and separated from the pack. He cruised into the end zone with the longest kickoff return in Super Bowl history. In the process, Howard sealed not only the Packers' first Super Bowl championship in three decades, but his own place in football lore.

New England PATRIOTS	14	0	7	0	21
Green Bay PACKERS	10	17	8	0	35

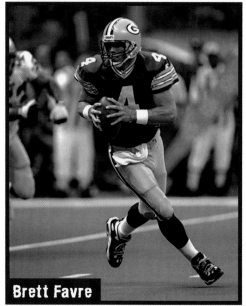

Brett Favre

SCORING

GB-Rison 54 pass from Favre (Jacke kick)
GB-FG Jacke 37
NE-Byars 1 pass from Bledsoe (Vinatieri kick)
NE-Coates 4 pass from Bledsoe (Vinatieri kick)
GB-Freeman 81 pass from Favre (Jacke kick)
GB-FG Jacke 31
GB-Favre 2 run (Jacke kick)
NE-Martin 18 run (Vinatieri kick)
GB-Howard 99 kick return (2-pt Chmura from Favre)

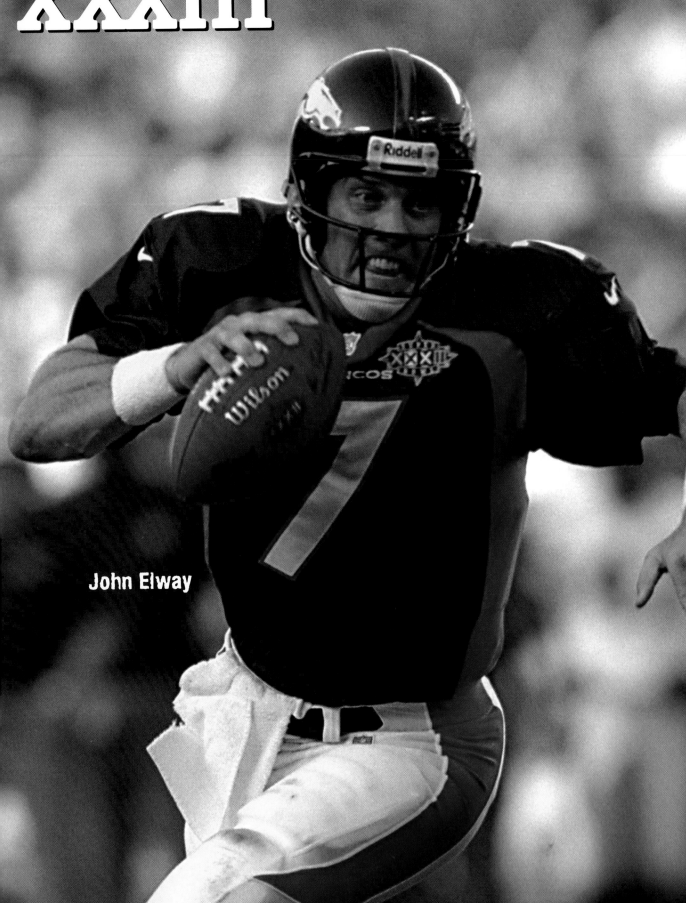

John Elway

Elway Goes Out in Style

LOOKING BACK NOW, it's hard to believe that John Elway was once considered by some to be a player who couldn't win the big game. No one ever questioned his talent or courage. Almost from the moment he entered the league, Elway was a prolific passer and confident field general. It's just that the Broncos kept getting to the Super Bowl— and losing! Three times in the 1980s Elway led the Broncos to the championship game, and three times he was denied a Super Bowl ring. A lesser player might have wilted under the weight of such disappointment. Not Elway. He kept coming back, and eventually his perseverance was rewarded. He led the Broncos to their first Super Bowl title in 1998, with a victory over the Green Bay Packers. One year later, in the final game of his long and illustrious career, Elway made it two in a row, as the Broncos defeated the Atlanta Falcons. Given the importance of the game and the way he played, it could be argued that Elway saved his best for last.

Rod Smith

At the relatively advanced age of 38, he played like a kid, completing 18 of 29 passes for 336 yards— the third-highest total in Super Bowl history. He ran for one touchdown and passed for another. To the surprise of absolutely no one, Elway was named the game's Most Valuable Player. Not only did he play flawlessly, but he also was responsible for the single biggest play in the game. It came late in the first half, with the Broncos nursing a 10–3 lead. After the Falcons missed an easy field goal, Denver took possession at its own 20-yard line. Elway wasted little time capitalizing on the Falcons' mistake. On the very next play, he threw a bomb to wide receiver Rod Smith, who never broke stride on his way to an 80-yard completion for a touchdown. Suddenly, the Broncos had a 17–3 lead. And they never looked back!

Denver BRONCOS	7	10	0	17	34
Atlanta FALCONS	3	3	0	13	19

SCORING

ATL-FG Andersen 32
DEN-Griffith 1 run (Elam kick)
DEN-FG Elam 26
DEN-R.Smith 80 pass from Elway (Elam kick)
ATL-FG Andersen 28
DEN-Griffith 1 run (Elam kick)
DEN-Elway 3 run (Elam kick)
ATL-Dwight 94 kickoff return (Andersen kick)
DEN-FG Elam 37
ATL-Mathis 3 pass from Chandler (pass failed)

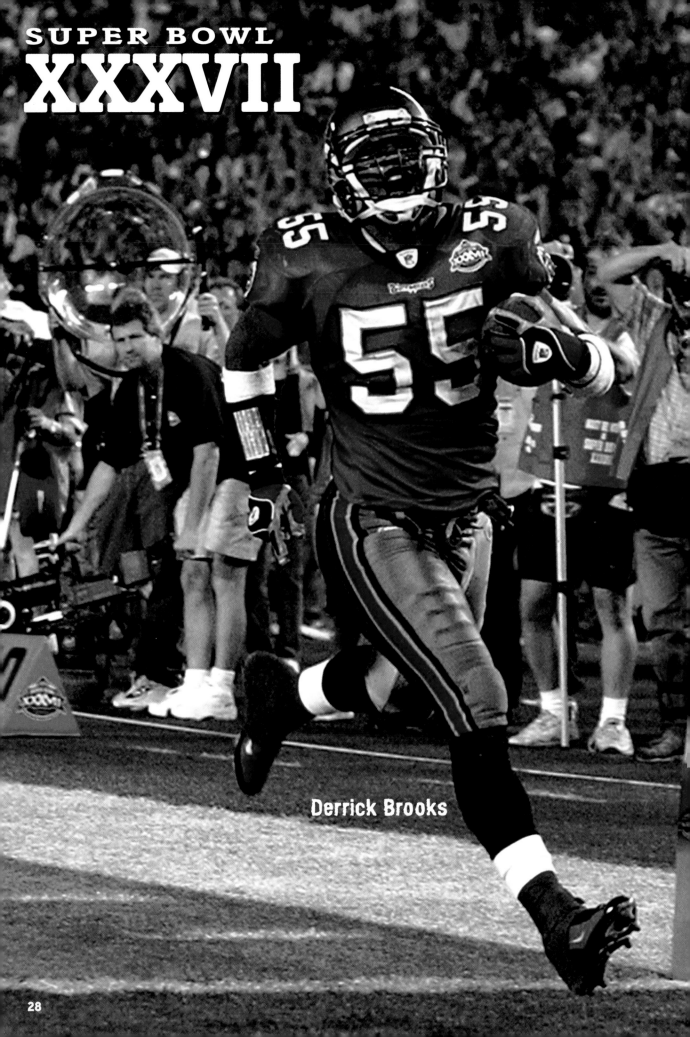

SUPER BOWL
XXXVII

Derrick Brooks

A Good Guy Gets It Done

IT WASN'T NECESSARILY THE MOST important play of the game, but it was one that lifted the hearts of Tampa Bay Buccaneers fans. On third-and-18, with the game already one-sided and just over a minute remaining, Raiders quarterback Rich Gannon dropped back to pass. As it had all evening, Tampa Bay's ferocious defense swarmed all over him, forcing Gannon to get rid of the ball in a hurry. The pass floated into the waiting arms of Tampa Bay linebacker Derrick Brooks, who raced 44 yards down the sideline for a touchdown, giving the Bucs an overwhelming 41–21 lead. With a wide smile visible through his facemask, Brooks was mobbed by his teammates. They were happy for him. After all, everyone likes to see the good guy get noticed. Not that Brooks hadn't been honored for his work. It's just that linebackers don't often find themselves in the end zone, holding the ball aloft. But it was appropriate that Brooks had his moment in the spotlight. The greatest sea-

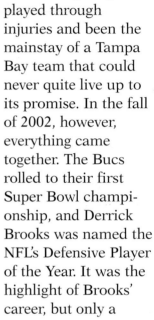

son in Tampa Bay history had been fueled in large part by his incomparable play. For several years Brooks had quietly played through injuries and been the mainstay of a Tampa Bay team that could never quite live up to its promise. In the fall of 2002, however, everything came together. The Bucs rolled to their first Super Bowl champi-onship, and Derrick Brooks was named the NFL's Defensive Player of the Year. It was the highlight of Brooks' career, but only a small fraction of what he has accom-plished both on and off the field. Not only has Derrick played in nine Pro Bowls, but he's also respected and admired for his tireless charitable work. Sometimes you have to wonder when Derrick finds time to sleep.

"Derrick is the kind of guy you want your kids to be like," says Tampa Bay coach Jon Gruden. "That's probably the best way I could describe him." And doesn't a guy like that deserve a touchdown on Super Bowl Sunday?

Oakland RAIDERS	3	0	6	12	21
Tampa Bay BUCCANEERS	3	17	14	14	48

SCORING

OAK-FG Janikowski 40
TB-FG Gramatica 31
TB-FG Gramatica 43
TB-Alstott 2 run (Gramatica kick)
TB-McCardell 5 pass from B. Johnson (Gramatica kick)
TB-McCardell 8 pass from B. Johnson (Gramatica kick)
TB-D.Smith 44 interception return (Gramatica kick)
OAK-Porter 39 pass from Gannon (pass failed)
OAK-E. Johnson 13 return of blocked punt (pass failed)
OAK-J.Rice 48 pass from Gannon (pass failed)
TB-Brooks 44 interception return (Gramatica kick)
TB-D.Smith 50 interception return (Gramatica kick)

Mike Vrabel

Vrabel Does It Again

TRIVIA QUESTION: Name any of the 14 players tied for sixth place on the list of career Super Bowl touchdown receptions. If you said John Taylor, a standout wide receiver for the San Francisco 49ers, you'd be right. If you mentioned former Dallas Cowboys superstar Michael Irvin, you'd also be right. In fact, the list is filled with the names of some of the NFL's great running backs and receivers. It also includes one linebacker: Mike Vrabel of the New England Patriots. If anyone thought Vrabel's touchdown reception in the Pats' Super Bowl victory over the Carolina Panthers in 2004 was a stunt, they were wrong. As Vrabel demonstrated the following year, in New England's triumph over the Eagles, this is a player whose versatility seems limitless. A defensive end during his collegiate career at Ohio State, Vrabel was moved to linebacker in the NFL, to make better use of his quickness. He became one of New England's most valuable defensive weapons, a player who could blitz the quarterback, chase down running backs, or defend receivers—all with equal success. And,

New England PATRIOTS	0	7	7	10	24
Philadephia EAGLES	0	7	7	7	21

sometimes, he would even join the offense, lining up at tight end in goal-line situations. Vrabel wasn't just a decoy, either. With great hands and a knack for finding a gap in the defensive coverage, he was a legitimate offensive threat. Just ask the Eagles! It was Vrabel who capped the opening drive of the second half with a juggling, off-balance catch that put the Patriots in front. The two-yard TD reception came despite the fact that Philadelphia defensive end Jevon Kearse had a handful of Vrabel's jersey. Vrabel was able to tip the pass from quarterback Tom Brady into the air and then pull the ball into his chest as he fell to the ground in the end zone. To give you some idea of how dangerous Vrabel is as a receiver, consider this: It was the fifth time in his career he had caught a pass. And his fifth touchdown! After the game, even Vrabel had a hard time comprehending his good fortune. "I'm still trying to believe it happened again," he said with a laugh. "I didn't expect it last year, and I didn't expect it this time." Maybe now, in the case of Mike Vrabel, it's time to expect the unexpected.

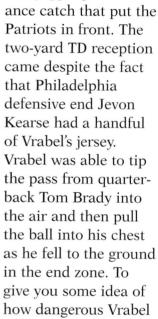

Tom Brady

SCORING

PHI-Smith 6 pass from McNabb (Akers kick)
NE-Givens 4 pass from Brady (Vinatieri kick)
NE-Vrabel 2 pass from Brady (Vinatieri kick)
PHI-Westbrook 10 pass from McNabb (Akers kick)
NE-Dillon 2 run (Vinatieri kick)
NE-FG Vinatieri 22
PHI-G.Lewis 30 pass from McNabb (Akers kick)

Super Bowl Results

I
JANUARY 15, 1967
GREEN BAY PACKERS 35
KANSAS CITY CHIEFS 10

II
JANUARY 14, 1968
GREEN BAY PACKERS 33
OAKLAND RAIDERS 14

III
JANUARY 12, 1969
NEW YORK JETS 16
BALTIMORE COLTS 7

IV
JANUARY 11, 1970
KANSAS CITY CHIEFS 23
MINNESOTA VIKINGS 7

V
JANUARY 17, 1971
BALTIMORE COLTS 16
DALLAS COWBOYS 13

VI
JANUARY 16, 1972
DALLAS COWBOYS 24
MIAMI DOLPHINS 3

VII
JANUARY 14, 1973
MIAMI DOLPHINS 14
WASHINGTON REDSKINS 7

VIII
JANUARY 13, 1974
MIAMI DOLPHINS 24
MINNESOTA VIKINGS 7

IX
JANUARY 12, 1975
PITTSBURGH STEELERS 16
MINNESOTA VIKINGS 6

X
JANUARY 18, 1976
PITTSBURGH STEELERS 21
DALLAS COWBOYS 17

XI
JANUARY 9, 1977
OAKLAND RAIDERS 32
MINNESOTA VIKINGS 14

XII
JANUARY 15, 1978
DALLAS COWBOYS 27
DENVER BRONCOS 10

XIII
JANUARY 21, 1979
PITTSBURGH STEELERS 35
DALLAS COWBOYS 31

XIV
JANUARY 20, 1980
PITTSBURGH STEELERS 31
LOS ANGELES RAMS 19

XV
JANUARY 25, 1981
OAKLAND RAIDERS 27
PHILADELPHIA EAGLES 10

XVI
JANUARY 24, 1982
SAN FRANCISCO 49ERS 26
CINCINNATI BENGALS 21

XVII
JANUARY 30, 1983
WASHINGTON REDSKINS 27
MIAMI DOLPHINS 17

XVIII
JANUARY 22, 1984
LOS ANGELES RAIDERS 38
WASHINGTON REDSKINS 9

XIX
JANUARY 20, 1985
SAN FRANCISCO 49ERS 38
MIAMI DOLPHINS 16

XX
JANUARY 26, 1986
CHICAGO BEARS 46
NEW ENGLAND PATRIOTS 10

XXI
JANUARY 25, 1987
NEW YORK GIANTS 39
DENVER BRONCOS 20

XXII
JANUARY 31, 1988
WASHINGTON REDSKINS 42
DENVER BRONCOS 10

XXIII
JANUARY 22, 1989
SAN FRANCISCO 49ERS 20
CINCINNATI BENGALS 16

XXIV
JANUARY 28, 1990
SAN FRANCISCO 49ERS 55
DENVER BRONCOS 10

XXV
JANUARY 27, 1991
NEW YORK GIANTS 20
BUFFALO BILLS 19

XXVI
JANUARY 26, 1992
WASHINGTON REDSKINS 37
BUFFALO BILLS 24

XXVII
JANUARY 31, 1993
DALLAS COWBOYS 52
BUFFALO BILLS 17

XXVIII
JANUARY 30, 1994
DALLAS COWBOYS 30
BUFFALO BILLS 13

XXIX
JANUARY 29, 1995
SAN FRANCISCO 49ERS 49
SAN DIEGO CHARGERS 26

XXX
JANUARY 28, 1996
DALLAS COWBOYS 27
PITTSBURGH STEELERS 17

XXXI
JANUARY 26, 1997
GREEN BAY PACKERS 35
NEW ENGLAND PATRIOTS 21

XXXII
JANUARY 25, 1998
DENVER BRONCOS 31
GREEN BAY PACKERS 24

XXXIII
JANUARY 31, 1999
DENVER BRONCOS 34
ATLANTA FALCONS 19

XXXIV
JANUARY 30, 2000
ST. LOUIS RAMS 23
TENNESSEE TITANS 16

XXXV
JANUARY 28, 2001
BALTIMORE RAVENS 34
NEW YORK GIANTS 7

XXXVI
FEBRUARY 3, 2002
NEW ENGLAND PATRIOTS 20
ST. LOUIS RAMS 17

XXXVII
JANUARY 26, 2003
TAMPA BAY BUCCANEERS 48
OAKLAND RAIDERS 21

XXXVIII
FEBRUARY 1, 2004
NEW ENGLAND PATRIOTS 32
CAROLINA PANTHERS 29

XXXIX
FEBRUARY 6, 2005
NEW ENGLAND PATRIOTS 24
PHILADELPHIA EAGLES 21

XL
FEBRUARY 5, 2006
PITTSBURGH STEELERS 21
SEATTLE SEAHAWKS 10